AF207024

SMARTPHONES
AND SOCIETY

How Do Smartphones Affect Social Interaction?

By Donna B. McKinney

ReferencePoint
Press®

San Diego, CA

For more information, contact:
ReferencePoint Press, Inc.
PO Box 27779
San Diego, CA 92198
www.ReferencePointPress.com

LIBRARY OF CONGRESS CATALOGING-IN-PUBLICATION DATA.

Names: McKinney, Donna B., author.
Title: How do smartphones affect social interaction? / by Donna B. McKinney.
Description: San Diego, CA : ReferencePoint Press, [2021] | Series: Smartphones and society | Includes bibliographical references and index.
Identifiers: LCCN 2020002874 (print) | LCCN 2020002875 (eBook) | ISBN 9781682829455 (hardcover) | ISBN 9781682829462 (pdf)
Subjects: LCSH: Cell phones and teenagers--Juvenile literature. | Interpersonal communication--Juvenile literature. | Social interaction--Juvenile literature. | Smartphones--Social aspects--Juvenile literature.
Classification: LCC HQ799.2.C45 M35 2021 (print) | LCC HQ799.2.C45 (eBook) | DDC 303.48/33--dc23
LC record available at https://lccn.loc.gov/2020002874
LC eBook record available at https://lccn.loc.gov/2020002875

CONTENTS

INTRODUCTION

SMARTPHONES AND SOCIAL INTERACTIONS 4

CHAPTER ONE

DO SMARTPHONES AFFECT USERS' INTERACTIONS? 10

CHAPTER TWO

HOW DO SMARTPHONES AFFECT USERS' DAILY LIVES? 24

CHAPTER THREE

HOW DO SMARTPHONES AFFECT COMMUNITIES? 38

CHAPTER FOUR

HOW CAN PEOPLE CONTROL THEIR SMARTPHONE USE? ... 54

SOURCE NOTES 70
FOR FURTHER RESEARCH 74
INDEX 76
IMAGE CREDITS 79
ABOUT THE AUTHOR 80

SMARTPHONES AND SOCIAL INTERACTIONS

Jason's smartphone buzzed, jolting him awake. He tapped his phone to silence his alarm. While still in bed, he checked his texts. He saw one new text sent this morning from his friend, Andrea. Andrea asked whether their history class quiz was today or Friday. He texted a quick reply: "Friday." Then his feet hit the floor, and he dressed for school. He took a photo of his dog as he ate his cereal. He shared the photo with his friends through the Snapchat app. Then he slipped his phone into the pocket of his jeans and headed to school.

When Jason arrived at school, he turned off his phone. He tucked it inside his backpack. Jason's school had a "no phones" rule. This meant that all students had to keep their

phones turned off and out of sight until the dismissal bell rang at the end of the school day.

After school, Jason sent a group text to his friends to find out where they wanted to hang out. They decided to go to a skateboard park. But when they got together, they spent most of their time checking the social media apps on their phones. Jason used his phone to take a video of his friend Sam trying a new trick on his skateboard and failing.

Most US teens who own smartphones text daily. They typically check social media apps multiple times each day.

Jason uploaded the video to the Instagram app on his phone. His phone immediately sounded with dings as his friends liked his post.

Later, during dinnertime, Jason tucked his phone into his pocket. His parents' rule was that none of them could look at their phones while at the dinner table. They wanted to have a conversation without distractions. Jason felt his phone vibrate in his pocket a couple of times during dinner.

He tried to sneak a peek to see who was texting him, but his dad caught him with his phone in his hand. Jason reluctantly handed his phone to his dad while his mom reviewed the family rules for a screen-free dinner.

When dinner was over, Jason got his phone back. He used the FaceTime app on his phone to video chat with his older brother. His brother was away at college. Jason liked catching up with his brother. They FaceTimed twice each week. Their smartphones made it easy to chat at any time.

SMARTPHONES EVERYWHERE

Smartphone users spend a significant amount of time on their devices each day. Valentina Rotondi is a sociologist and a researcher at the University of Oxford. In a 2017 research article, she and her fellow researchers wrote, "Estimates suggest that people spend on average up to five hours per day on their smartphone . . . with the device being the first thing people look at in the morning and the last thing they look at before going to sleep."[1]

Smartphones play a major role in people's daily lives. People rely on smartphones to connect

"Estimates suggest that people spend on average up to five hours per day on their smartphone . . . with the device being the first thing people look at in the morning and the last thing they look at before going to sleep."[1]

—Valentina Rotondi, a researcher at the University of Oxford

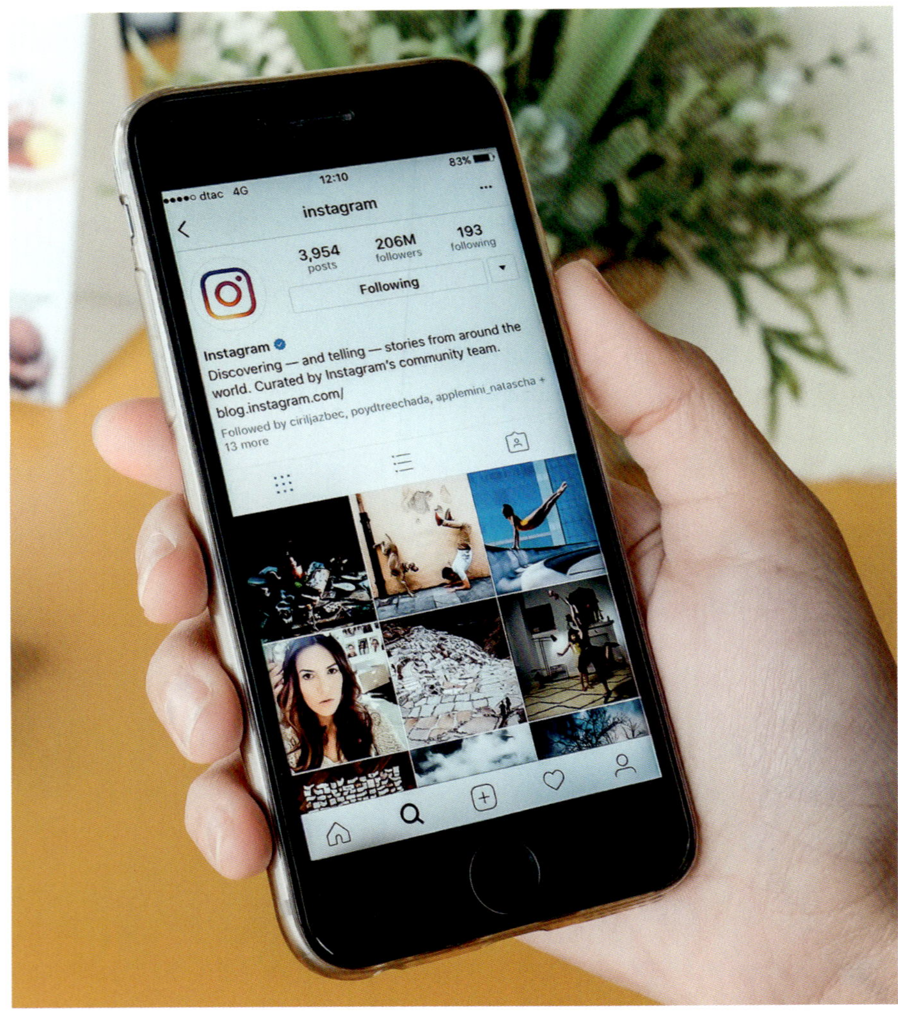

Instagram is one of the most popular social media platforms among US teens. Users can alter their photos to make attractive images.

to each other. At the same time, smartphones come with many apps and can be powerful distractions. They can interrupt or get in the way of real-life interactions. Jean Twenge is a psychology professor at San Diego State University. She found that smartphones can reduce people's happiness when they interrupt or distract from in-person conversations. She said, "Whether it's someone you've never met or it's friends and family, spending time with people face to face is linked with happiness."[2]

Darlene McLaughlin is an assistant professor at the Texas A&M Health Science Center College of Medicine. She studies how people's behaviors can affect their physical and mental health. She described a phenomenon called fear of missing out (FOMO). FOMO is caused by people's constant connections to social media, often through smartphones. People often post attractive photos of their lives on social media. Others who see these photos may feel envious. McLaughlin says, "This constant fear of missing out means you are not participating as a real person in your own world."[3]

Ethan Kross is a professor of psychology at the University of Michigan. He says, "There are helpful or harmful ways of navigating the offline world, and the same is true of the digital world."[4] There are strategies people can utilize to manage their smartphone use. That way, smartphones can become useful tools rather than devices that control or dominate their lives.

CHAPTER ONE

DO SMARTPHONES AFFECT USERS' INTERACTIONS?

For today's teenagers, smartphones have always existed. While many parents and grandparents can recall the days before they had smartphones, teenagers only know a world where smartphones have always been available. The smartphone is a powerful tool with many useful functions and features. But like many things in life, smartphone use can have both positive and negative effects.

SMARTPHONE TOOLS

Smartphones can help make people's lives easier and more efficient. With a smartphone in hand, teens can track their class assignments, read the news, take photos, call a friend, or send an email. People can also use smartphones to do online banking, check social media, or find their

Most teen smartphone users in the United States prefer to communicate with their friends through text messages. Teens who have smartphones are more likely to communicate daily with their best friends than teens who do not have smartphones.

way home with a map app. Many smartphone apps are useful tools. For example, some apps provide a flashlight, a calculator, a compass, or an alarm clock. Smartphone users can also find gaming apps for entertainment. Other types of apps make communication easier. Family members and friends who are separated by great distances can call or use text or video chat apps to communicate.

Many people use their smartphones to video chat. Popular video chat apps include Skype and FaceTime.

Social media and messaging apps can also connect people from across the country and around the world.

But there are negatives that come with the convenience and efficiency the smartphone brings. Researcher Valentina Rotondi explains, "[The smartphone] can simultaneously satisfy the need to make a phone call, take a photo, pay a bill, listen to music, watch a video, use the Internet, chat through social networks and, more generally, be entertained. All these functions have substantially improved and simplified life. However, the very fact that these activities can be carried out anywhere, has made this technology more intrusive than any other."[5]

Because smartphones are handheld computers, they are easy to carry. People can hold them in their hands, put them in a pocket, or slip them into a bag. This accessibility makes it easy for smartphones to interfere with people's daily activities, including their interactions with other people. Whether at school, home, or work, a person's smartphone is often within reach.

SMARTPHONE DEPENDENCY

Many researchers are studying the influence smartphones have on people's lives. According to Rotondi, studies show that "the smartphone has dramatically changed our daily life and, in particular, how we interact with others. These changes have made life easier in many respects. Yet, they did not come without costs."[6] Rotondi and other researchers have found that there can be negative consequences to smartphone use. Many smartphone users have some awareness of these consequences. They understand the disruption that comes with having constant access to a smartphone. In 2018, the Pew Research Center surveyed US teens on their cell phone use.

TECHNOFERENCE

Social scientists created a name to describe the interference of technology in people's lives. They call this disruption "technoference." Brandon McDaniel, a scientist at Illinois State University, explained that technoference is "a term that deals with the everyday very minor sorts of intrusions, interruptions that our technology devices may [create]." McDaniel and his research team studied parents who had children aged five years old or younger. They looked at 170 families. They observed the ways cell phones and other devices disrupted the parents' interactions with their children. The researchers discovered that when parents had a hard time managing their own phone use, it impacted their relationships with their children and was linked to misbehavior in the children. Technoference can also affect people's relationships with other family members and friends. In addition, the pull of smartphones and other devices can disrupt people's sleep and reduce their productivity at work.

Quoted in "Technoference?" Child Trends, *January 2018. www.childtrends.org.*

Fifty-four percent of the respondents worried that they spent too much time on their cell phones. Common Sense Media conducted a survey of 1,141 US teens in the same year. Forty-seven percent of those who had smartphones said they were addicted to their phones.

Many smartphone users connect with each other through their phones. When these people do not have access to their phones, they may feel like they are isolated or cut off from social connections. This makes them anxious and uneasy. Researchers use the word "nomophobia" to describe this feeling. The term is shorthand for "no mobile phone phobia." A phobia is a strong and irrational fear of something. Nomophobia can make it difficult for people to focus on the in-person conversations and activity happening around them.

In the 2018 Pew Research Center survey of US teens, 56 percent of the respondents said being away from their phone makes them feel anxious, lonely, or upset. Nicholas Carr is a writer who covers technology and culture. He says, "I think we know enough now to be deeply concerned about how these very, very powerful and seductive devices are influencing pretty much every aspect of our [lives]."[7]

THE PULL TO CONNECT

Scientists have an explanation for why smartphones are so appealing. Humans are hardwired to connect with other people. It is because of this desire to connect that the pull of the smartphone is almost irresistible.

Throughout history, humans have depended on close relationships with other people. People have been drawn to each other, forming relationships that bring both joy and safety. These relationships were built around networks of family and close friends. In these networks, people trusted each other and worked together. They relied on each other to survive. Hundreds of years ago, these social networks were made up of people who lived physically close together as neighbors in villages and towns. Today, smartphones can help users expand their social networks. Smartphone users can reach and connect to people around the world.

David Sbarra is a psychology professor at the University of Arizona. He explains, "The draw or pull of a smartphone is connected to very old [parts of] the brain that were critical to our survival, and central to the ways we connect with others are self-disclosure and responsiveness."[8] One of the smartphone's primary benefits is that it provides humans with another way to connect to one another, answering that deep desire people have to develop and maintain social networks.

THE DRAWBACKS

Even though many teens understand the negative consequences related to smartphone use, they also experience the advantages of having a smartphone. The social media they access through their smartphones pulls at them in both positive and negative ways. In the 2018 Common Sense Media survey, 25 percent of the respondents said using social media makes them feel less lonely. Yet a few of the respondents said using social media

People who are addicted to their smartphones may not be aware of how their phone use affects their relationships. Approximately half of US teen smartphone users say they use their phones too much.

makes them feel lonelier. The use of social media can lead to feelings of loneliness when people neglect their in-person friendships. People's relationships with family and friends can become strained if they spend too much time online or on apps.

That same smartphone that helps people connect to each other can also distract them from their in-person relationships and conversations. When two people are trying to have a face-to-face conversation, it can be challenging when one person has his head down and his eyes fixed on a smartphone screen. With a smartphone in hand, it is very easy to be mentally checked out from everything else that is happening. People focus on their phones and tune out the activity around them. This distraction can lead to conflict between family members and friends.

Science journalist Yudhijit Bhattacharjee summarized the findings scientists are uncovering as they dig deeper into the question of how smartphones affect users' social lives:

The constant connectivity and access to information that smartphones offer have made the devices something of a drug for hundreds of millions of users. Scientists are just beginning to research this phenomenon, but their studies suggest that we are becoming increasingly distracted, spending less time in the real world and being drawn more deeply into the virtual world.[9]

In earlier generations, many teenagers did not have smartphones. Smartphones did not become popular and widely available until the 2010s. Because of the smartphone and other modern technologies, today's teens socialize in very different ways than teens did in the past. Psychology professor Jean Twenge reported, "The number of teens who get together with their friends nearly every day dropped by more than 40 percent from 2000 to 2015."[10] Smartphones may have played a role in this change. This shift happened as smartphones became more widely popular.

Research has shown that face-to-face relationships typically last longer and are more fulfilling and valuable than online relationships. In an in-person conversation, people can observe nonverbal cues such as eye contact and

THE SIMON PERSONAL COMMUNICATOR

The computer and technology company International Business Machines (IBM) developed the first cell phone with smart capabilities in 1992. IBM called the device the Simon Personal Communicator. The Simon was offered for sale to the public in 1994. This device functioned as a cell phone with some added features. It had a touchscreen. Its features included an address book, a calendar, a clock, and a scheduler for appointments. The Simon did not have a web browser to surf the internet, but it could send and receive emails and faxes. This email access made the Simon appealing to buyers. Buyers did not call the Simon a "smartphone." This term would not be used until 1995.

The Simon would be considered large and clunky by today's standards. It was 8 inches (20 cm) long, 2.5 inches (6.4 cm) wide, and 1.5 inches (3.8 cm) thick. Its battery only lasted about one hour, which was a drawback for users. The Simon only stayed on the market for about six months.

body language. These nonverbal cues are another level of communication. They help people connect with each other. They can communicate a person's mood or feelings as well as or better than what the person says. With the exception of video chat, people cannot observe nonverbal cues in online conversations.

Twenge studies teens as part of her research. One of these teens was a thirteen-year-old girl named Athena who lived in Texas. Twenge talked to Athena in 2016. Twenge remembered how she used to shop at a mall with her friends during her middle school years in the 1980s. Twenge asked Athena whether she and her friends went to shopping malls in their free time. Athena said that she and her friends did not go to the mall very often. Instead, they spent much of their free time communicating through their phones. Twenge observed,

> *Unlike the teens of my generation, who might have spent an evening tying up the family landline with gossip, [today's teens] talk on Snapchat, the smartphone app that allows users to send pictures and videos that quickly disappear. They make sure to keep up their Snapstreaks, which show how many days in a row they have Snapchatted with each other.*[11]

Athena told Twenge that she spent most of her summer vacation alone in her bedroom with her smartphone. "We didn't have a choice to know any life without iPads or iPhones," Athena said. "I think we like our phones more than we like actual people."[12]

Researchers have also discovered that some people use their smartphones to avoid interacting with others. Results from the 2018 Pew Research Center survey showed that about 43 percent of US teens often or sometimes use their phones to avoid social interactions. They use their phones while around other people so they appear distracted. That way, people do not approach them and try to talk to them.

THE INFLUENCE OF SMARTPHONES

In her research, Twenge found many differences between young people today and earlier generations of teens. These differences are evident in the way today's teens view the world and how they spend their time. Twenge pinpoints the dramatic shifts in behavior to the year 2012. In that year, the proportion of Americans who owned smartphones surpassed 50 percent.

HOW TEENS USE CELL PHONES

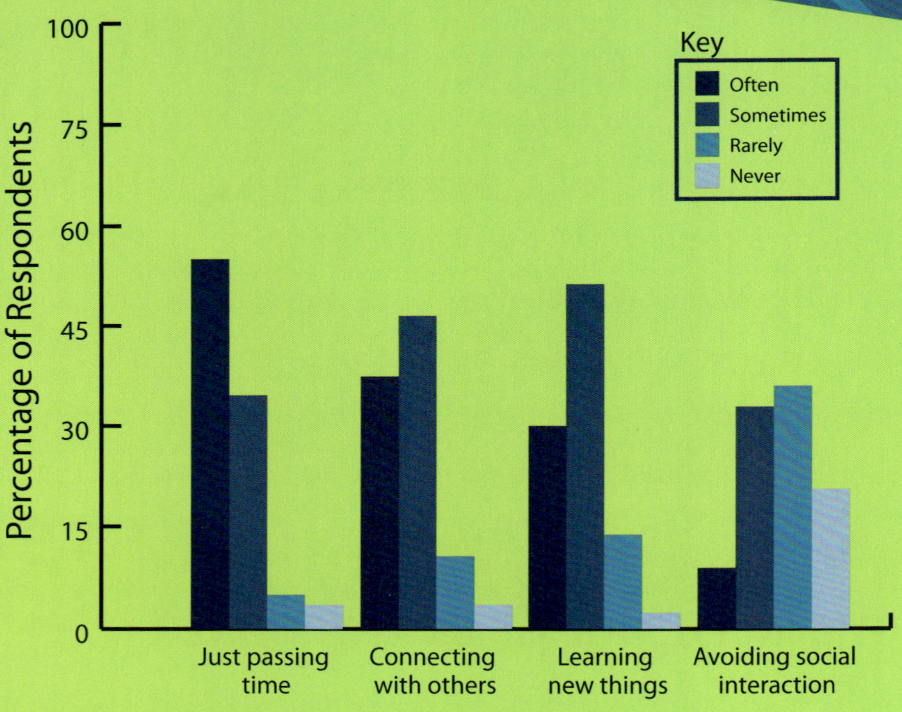

This graph shows the results of a Pew Research Center survey that was conducted in 2018. Researchers asked a group of US teens about the reasons they use their cell phones. The respondents were between the ages of thirteen and seventeen.

Katherine Schaeffer, "Most US Teens Who Use Cellphones Do It to Pass Time, Connect with Others, Learn New Things," Pew Research Center, *August 23, 2019. www.pewresearch.org.*

When smartphones and tablets were first developed in the 1990s, people began to wonder about the negative effects of time spent looking at a screen. Still, Twenge explained, "The impact of these devices has not been fully appreciated, and goes far beyond the usual concerns about curtailed attention spans."[13]

Many people's lives changed after the smartphone was created. The smartphone allowed them to connect to others in new ways. It altered the ways in which they communicated. Teens across the United States were especially drawn to smartphones. Twenge said, "Where there are cell towers, there are teens living their lives on their smartphone."[14]

In many ways, smartphones make communication easier and more efficient. However, they can also act as a distraction that keeps people from developing meaningful connections. Meaningful social connections enhance people's emotional health and well-being. Smartphone users can work to build healthy relationships with family and friends both in real life and through the use of technology. People can learn how to successfully navigate their relationships with their smartphones in hand.

CHAPTER TWO

HOW DO SMARTPHONES AFFECT USERS' DAILY LIVES?

Because many people use their smartphones every day, these devices have become an important part of people's routines. Smartphones can influence and interfere with many parts of users' daily lives. In particular, research has shown that smartphones have a strong effect on people's social interactions. Researcher Valentina Rotondi says, "The advent of the smartphone has changed substantially the way we access information, allocate time and interact with others."[15] Rotondi acknowledged that

"The advent of the smartphone has changed substantially the way we access information, allocate time and interact with others."[15]

—Valentina Rotondi, a researcher at the University of Oxford

Smartphones can capture images of important social events such as vacations. Smartphones can store and organize thousands of images.

smartphones have made people's lives easier in many ways. But she also noted that many people rely on or are addicted to their smartphones. Smartphone overuse can have negative effects.

CLOSE BUT DISTANT

Smartphones can empower people in many ways. These devices allow people to gather information easily and work from any location. Friends can contact each other quickly and coordinate plans. In this way, smartphones can bring people together. "However," Rotondi explains, "while the smartphone can bring distant people closer together, at least virtually, it can also make close people more distant."[16] In this instance, "close people" means people who are near each other. In many crowded areas or settings, such as shopping malls or school bus stops, people can often be seen standing close to each other but with their heads tucked down and their eyes glued to a smartphone screen. The pull of a smartphone can be hard to resist. Just from

PHUBBING

The term "phone snubbing," or "phubbing," describes the act of using a smartphone to ignore other people. This term first came into use in 2012. Some people might view phubbing as just an annoying habit. However, psychologist Emma Seppälä believes it can have negative consequences. She said, "Ironically, phubbing is meant to connect you, presumably, with someone through social media or texting. But it actually can severely disrupt your present-moment, in-person relationships." Some researchers have also found that phubbing can have a negative effect on the phone user's mental health. Experts have discovered that eye contact is the most essential form of connection between two people. Posture and facial expressions are also important. These nonverbal cues communicate a person's attitude better than the person's words. People who phub focus on their phone screens instead of making eye contact with other people. This behavior harms their in-person connections.

Quoted in Jamie Ducharme, "'Phubbing' Is Hurting Your Relationships. Here's What It Is," Time, *March 29, 2018. www.time.com.*

casual observation, it is easy to see that smartphones influence people's interactions or lack thereof.

Smartphone users can silence their phones so they do not hear notification alerts. However, researchers have found that this action often does not make smartphones less distracting. Researchers observed that even when people have their phones in silent mode, they still feel the need to be constantly connected to others. Experts call this state "absent presence." Absent presence decreases the quality of in-person conversations. When people are holding a smartphone but not using it, their attention is still pulled away from these conversations. They withdraw from the relationships that are right in front of them.

Researchers at the University of Essex conducted experiments to learn more about absent presence. The researchers set up an experiment where two people sat in a room talking to each other. In some cases, the researchers placed a smartphone on a table beside the participants. They found that even when the phone was in silent mode, the participants had less meaningful conversations with the phone present than when there was no phone in the room. The researchers concluded that smartphones have the power to disrupt social interactions just by their presence in a room.

Imagine a busy station where planes, trains, and buses are constantly arriving and departing. Many people are coming and going from the station, and the busyness can feel overwhelming. In a similar way, someone who has a smartphone feels the presence of a constant flow of information. The opportunity for communication with others is always present when a smartphone is near. At times, that overload of communication and information can be exhausting. When people feel preoccupied or overwhelmed, they are distracted from their in-person conversations.

In 2018, two researchers from the University of Kent's School of Psychology conducted a study. Their study involved 153 participants. The researchers showed the participants videos of two people interacting. They asked the participants to imagine themselves as one of the people in the conversation. In some of the videos, one person was focusing on a smartphone and completely ignoring the other person. In other videos, there were no distractions. After participants watched a video, the researchers asked them a series of questions. Participants who had watched videos where one person was ignored reported lower levels of belonging and self-esteem.

Rotondi and her research team have also studied the effects of smartphones on in-person interactions.

The researchers found that when people spend more time on their smartphones and less time talking to friends in person, they feel less satisfaction with their friends. Researchers have also found a connection between time spent with friends and overall life satisfaction. People who spend more time with their friends are more likely to report

Some smartphone users bully or exclude others through text messaging or social media. Kids who have cell phones are more likely to be bullies or get bullied than kids who do not have cell phones.

a greater sense of satisfaction with their lives than those who spend less time with friends. So smartphone overuse may lead not only to decreased satisfaction with friends but also to decreased satisfaction with life in general. Rotondi reported, "Our findings indicate that time spent with friends is worth less, in terms of life satisfaction, for individuals who use the smartphone."[17] Rotondi and other researchers look forward to further study where they can explore how people adapt to the useful features of smartphone technology without letting these devices impact their relationships in negative ways. Adam Gazzaley is a neuroscientist at the University of California, San Francisco. He says, "The crux of the problem is figuring out how to get all these amazing benefits of this globally interconnected world without abandoning the things that make us most human."[18]

DON'T FORGET YOUR MANNERS

Smartphones are useful in many ways. But a reliance on these devices can lead to addiction. Psychologist Suzana E. Flores says,

> *Of course, there's the addiction aspect—*
> *[smartphones are] always within arm's reach.*
> *We should continue to enjoy our digital connections,*
> *but second only to our offline realities. Just as with*
> *anything else, too much of a good thing may not be a*
> *good thing after all.*[19]

Flores believes enjoying the smartphone is fine, but the online connections people develop should not take the place of their in-person relationships. Flores has found that people tend to forget their manners when they are using a smartphone. They focus on the phone while ignoring the friend in the room with them.

Scientists have found that people get a dopamine rush when they receive notifications on their phones. Dopamine is a chemical that is produced in a person's brain. When large amounts of dopamine are released, a person feels a rush of pleasure and happiness. Eating and exercising are activities that can cause a release of dopamine. Harmful behaviors such as drug and alcohol use can trigger a release of dopamine too. People seek out these substances because of the dopamine rush they get. Then they can become addicted to these substances.

Dopamine also plays a role in smartphone addiction. Flores says, "The dopamine hits we receive every time we get a push notification may be to blame, so much so that many of us have convinced ourselves that our push notifications are more important than who or what is around us."[20] Some experts see similarities between smartphone addiction and drug addiction. People who are addicted to substances may likewise ignore or abandon their personal relationships because the substance becomes more important. They may become socially isolated. When people who are addicted to a substance try to stop using it, they experience withdrawal symptoms. These symptoms include anger, anxiety, and depression. People who are addicted to smartphones experience similar symptoms when they are away from their phones for long periods of time.

WHEN THE SMARTPHONE GOES TO DINNER

Some people have explored how smartphones can affect social interactions during mealtimes. Elizabeth Dunn and Ryan Dwyer are researchers at the University of British Columbia. They explored how much people enjoy spending time with each other when a smartphone is present. Dwyer said,

> *You see people in restaurants all the time who are sitting across the table from each other, and instead of staring at each other, they're staring at their phones. We were really curious: Is it having an impact on people's social interactions, how much they're enjoying the time they're spending with other people?*[21]

Dunn and Dwyer's study involved 300 people. The researchers asked these people to go out and eat a meal with family or friends. The participants did not realize the purpose of the study. The researchers disguised the study's purpose so it would not affect the participants' responses. The researchers instructed half of the participants to put their phones out on the table while they ate their meal. They told these participants that they would receive a text with a question about the study sometime during the meal. The researchers asked the other participants to put their devices away. These participants expected to get a paper with a question about the study sometime during the meal. Afterward, all of the participants answered questions about how much they enjoyed their meal.

Dunn and Dwyer found that the participants who had their phones out on the table used their phones for about 11 percent of the overall mealtime. This phone use contributed to a decrease in enjoyment for both the participants and their family and friends. With technology

Kids often observe and learn from their parents' behaviors. Kids whose parents are addicted to smartphones are more likely to become addicted to the devices themselves.

at the table, people felt more distracted and less socially engaged. The researchers concluded that it is not likely that the presence of a smartphone will ruin a person's dinner, but there is a good chance it will decrease a person's satisfaction.

PHONES AND RELATIONSHIPS

Some scientists are studying how smartphones affect romantic relationships. Their findings show that smartphones can have a negative effect on these relationships. For example, researchers from Baylor University surveyed 453 US adults in 2015. They asked participants how often their partners used their phones and ignored them. Then they asked participants about their satisfaction with these relationships. Those who reported that their partners used smartphones often were more likely to say that they were unhappy with their relationships.

Psychology professor David Sbarra has reviewed several of these studies. He noted that smartphones can significantly interfere with many types of relationships. He says, "When you are distracted into or by the device, then your attention is divided, and being responsive to our partners—an essential ingredient for building intimacy—requires attention in the here and now."[22]

James A. Roberts is a professor of marketing at Baylor University. He was one of the researchers involved in the 2015 Baylor

University survey. He studies how people interact with technology. He is also the author of the book *Too Much of a Good Thing: Are You Addicted to Your Smartphone?* He recommends that families set aside times during the day when they do not use their phones. He says, "The more precious your time is, the more you need to be vigilant about how you spend it."[23] He called it rude behavior when people are together but constantly checking or texting on their smartphones. This behavior can ultimately damage the quality of people's relationships.

CHAPTER THREE

HOW DO SMARTPHONES AFFECT COMMUNITIES?

When thinking about how smartphones affect social interactions, it is helpful to look at both individuals and communities as a whole. It is clear that smartphones have an impact, both positive and negative, on people's social interactions. Smartphones also influence communities in many ways.

David Sbarra studies smartphones' effects on relationships and social interactions. He said, "Between 2000 and 2018, we've seen the largest technological advances, arguably, at any point in the last one hundred years. We are interested in understanding the role of social

In the United States, many families have multiple devices in their household. Smartphones are the most common type of device.

relationships in human well-being. We can understand this from the level of what individuals do in relationships, but we can also understand it at the level of societal changes and societal forces that may push on relationships."[24] Sbarra and his fellow researchers are exploring how new technologies and devices such as smartphones shape communities.

Smartphone use can have a contagious effect in group settings. When one person starts checking his

"Between 2000 and 2018, we've seen the largest technological advances, arguably, at any point in the last one hundred years."[24]

—David Sbarra, professor of psychology at the University of Arizona or her phone, other people in the group are more likely to check their phones too. Author and researcher James A. Roberts calls this behavior "cellularitis." He explains that people may feel ignored or offended when others around them are looking at phones. In response, people may pull out their phones to appear as if they are also uninterested in conversation. Roberts says, "When other people use their cell phones, we do it too in self-defense."[25]

Researchers have observed that smartphones can have an influence even in casual encounters, such as those people might have on the street or in other public places. Science journalist Lynne Peeples writes,

> *Even basic human decency may be sacrificed. Research suggests that smartphones can inhibit people from offering help to strangers on the street, reduce how much we smile at unfamiliar faces in a waiting room and even lessen our trust of strangers, neighbors and people of other religions or nationalities.*[26]

For example, social psychologist Kostadin Kushlev conducted a study in 2018 that showed this effect. He found that when strangers who waited together had phones, they smiled at each other less often than if they did not have phones.

Peeples also writes,
"Perhaps not surprisingly,
researchers have also
begun to link weakened
social skills, including the
inability to read emotions or
initiate casual conversations,
to smartphone use."[27] Yalda
Uhls is a senior researcher at the University of California,
Los Angeles's Children's Digital Media Center. She explored
whether smartphone use affects people's social skills. She
observed preteens at a nature camp who did not have
access to smartphones or other technological devices
for five days. She compared this group to preteens who
had access to such devices. Uhls and her research team
concluded, "Our study suggests that skills in reading human
emotion may be diminished when children's face-to-face
interaction is displaced by technologically mediated
communication."[28]

In these important ways, smartphone use can influence
how people in communities relate to each other. It can
weaken people's communication skills. Researchers
have also found that, beyond these casual encounters,
smartphone use can affect people's interactions at work
and at school.

Many people use their smartphones while on public transportation to pass the time. As a result, they do not interact much with others in these settings.

IMPACT IN BUSINESS

Smartphones have changed how people interact in businesses and companies. Some work that used to be conducted in person can now be easily handled through use of a smartphone. People can place orders, schedule jobs, and do their banking through smartphone apps with little or no face-to-face human interaction required. This allows some business to be carried out more efficiently. For example, people can use smartphone apps to deposit checks even during the hours when their banks are closed.

No social interaction is required for this process. People can simply log into their bank accounts and upload photos of their checks. Then the checks are deposited.

Before the arrival of the smartphone, many employees worked only inside office buildings. They sat at desks and were surrounded by coworkers. Today, smartphones and other devices help employees do all kinds of work tasks while away from the office. They can send and receive work emails. They can also have meetings through videoconferencing apps on their phones. They can submit reports or file orders through phone apps too. Smartphones allow workers to do their jobs well and give them the

DAILY SMARTPHONE USE

Larry Rosen is an emeritus professor of psychology at California State University, Dominguez Hills. In 2016, he used an app to track how often a group of high school students and young adults used their smartphones. The app counted the number of times people unlocked their phones. Each participant in the study unlocked his or her phone an average of fifty-six times a day. Rosen and his team did a follow-up study in 2018. By then, this number had risen to an average of seventy-three times a day. The researchers believe this number is high because notifications, posts, and messages are like rewards. People like getting rewards, so they keep checking their email and social media.

In a different study, the software company Dscout conducted research to see how people used their smartphones. This study looked at how many times users tapped, swiped, or clicked on their phones. The results showed that each participant did these actions an average of 2,617 times each day.

freedom to work outside the office if needed. So while smartphones may reduce face-to-face interactions in the workplace, they also can help improve workers' efficiency and flexibility.

IMPACT ON SCHOOLS

Smartphones also influence people's interactions in schools and educational settings. Before the days of smartphones and other mobile devices, being absent from school usually meant falling behind in classwork for a while. Today, students can use smartphones to organize and track their assignments. That way, students who are absent can use smartphone apps to keep up with the work they miss. An app may send students a message or notification when an upcoming assignment is due. This process does not replace the learning and collaboration that goes on during in-class discussions, but it can ease the impact of missed days in class.

Some high school teachers use smartphones in their classrooms, especially when laptops are not readily available. Teachers may assign students to work in pairs so that everyone has access to a phone. Ken Halla, who teaches ninth-grade world history and government classes, regularly uses smartphones in his classroom. He says, "Not every classroom can get a laptop every day, so

Smartphones can be helpful tools for student group projects. Students can use them to look up information and stay connected with each other.

[devices like smartphones], even if you have to pair up, become something useful for teachers."[29]

Students can also use smartphones to enhance their learning or prepare for exams. Some smartphone apps are educational. They teach users about a variety of topics. Halla uses apps that are specifically designed for teaching social studies courses. For example, there is an app that educates users about US presidents, the White House, and the US constitution. Halla also uses a smartphone app that allows him to text questions to students before an

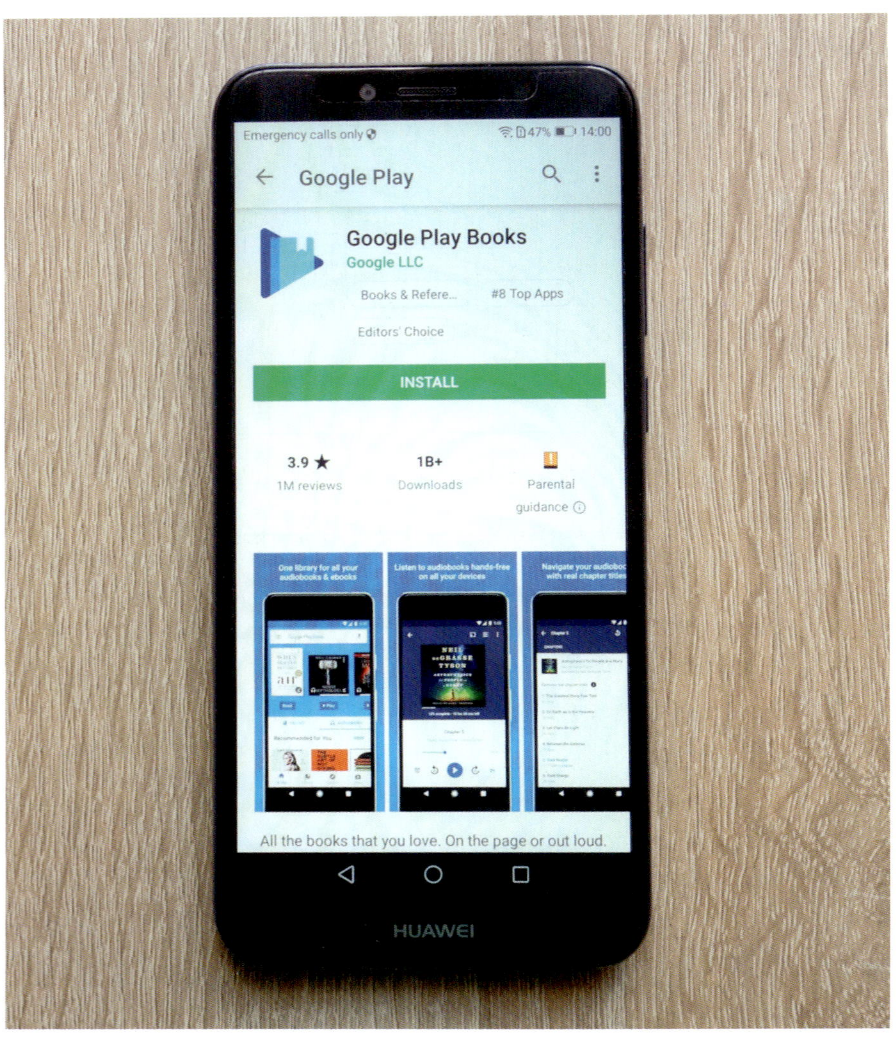

Smartphone users can read e-books through apps such as Google Play Books. Other apps allow users to check out audiobooks or e-books from a library.

upcoming test. He texts students questions based on the material he covers in class. Students text their responses to him. This helps students prepare for the test. It also helps Halla determine whether he is covering the subject matter well enough that most students understand it.

Teachers may use smartphones in the classroom in other ways too. Halla allows his students to put in earbuds and listen to music on their phones while working. He discovered that listening to music in this way helps many students be quieter and more focused while working. Halla says, "I've always been that type of person who likes to adapt and change as time goes on."[30]

Despite the potential usefulness of smartphones in school settings, these devices can be distractions that make it hard for students to pay attention. Students who have access to smartphones may try to check social media, text, or play games on their phones while in class. For this reason, some teachers and schools do not allow smartphones in classrooms.

However, smartphones may give students access to many educational materials that are not available at their local libraries. E-books and video lectures are widely available to students who have smartphones or other electronic devices. Students can interact with their teachers and classmates through smartphone apps. In these ways, smartphones can improve the learning process.

IMPACT IN HEALTH CARE

Smartphones have also had a tremendous impact in health care. People can use smartphones to manage their prescriptions, research treatment options, schedule appointments, review test results, and even track their health habits. Many health care–related tasks that used to require in-person interactions can now be handled using smartphone apps. Some of the personal connections have been removed while the process of gathering and tracking information has become more efficient.

Some people might think that talking to someone just to ask a question, schedule an appointment, or fill a prescription is a meaningless conversation. But researchers view these casual social interactions in a different way. Social psychologist Kostadin Kushlev says, "We actually get quite a lot from casual social interactions. Even when phones are at their most useful—such as when we're bored to death in the waiting room—there might be other things we're missing out on."[31] These missed benefits can include positive interactions and the development of new social connections.

RESOLVING CONFLICTS

In a 2018 Common Sense Media survey of more than 1,000 US teenagers, 27 percent of the respondents said social media was "extremely" or "very" important as a platform for their creative expression. Many people use social media to share artwork, photos, or other things that they like. Social media is easily accessible through smartphones. This type of sharing can create or enhance social interactions. However, some smartphone users increasingly rely on social media for

communication that would be more effective in person, such as arguments. Smartphones have changed how people deal with conflicts. Psychologist Suzana E. Flores is concerned that many smartphone users try to deal with personal disagreements through messaging apps instead of through meaningful, in-person conversations. She says,

> *In many ways, digital communication appears to be altering our comfort levels with direct and honest communication and conflict resolution. Doing so will inevitably negatively affect our relationships, since important discussions should be done in person or, at the very least, over the phone so that misunderstandings could be minimized.*[32]

SMARTPHONES USED BADLY

As handheld computers, smartphones provide users with easy access to the internet. The internet provides a wealth of information that can be useful, such as educational background on a topic. However, the internet also has information that can be harmful or dangerous, such as obscene or hate-filled content. In the 2018 Common Sense Media survey of US teenagers, 64 percent of the respondents said they had "often" or "sometimes" come across social media content that is racist, sexist, homophobic, or hateful toward certain religious groups. People who have smartphones are also more vulnerable to cyberstalking and cyberbullying.

GuardChild, an internet safety group, reported alarming statistics. It reviewed the results of several surveys of teen internet users in the United States. Approximately 20 percent of the respondents said they had received an unwanted sexual solicitation, such as a request for sexual activity, chat, or information. Approximately 69 percent of the respondents said they regularly receive online communications from strangers but do not tell their parents about it. These statistics point to the many possible dangerous social interactions that happen through the internet. The people who post this sexual content are predators trying to lure teens into dangerous situations. As a general rule, it is wise to be careful in all online social interactions. Also, when teens encounter people they do not know through the internet or through a smartphone app, they should use great caution and not be afraid to seek advice or help from a trusted adult. Reaching out to a parent, grandparent, teacher, or coach for help is wise with any online social interactions that make people feel uncomfortable.

CYBERBULLYING AND CYBERSTALKING

Cyberbullying happens when people use digital devices such as smartphones to bully others. Cyberbullying can happen online or through smartphone apps. People may send texts, emails, or messages that hurt or humiliate someone. Or they may create harmful social media posts that insult someone. In Common Sense Media's 2018 survey of US teens, about one in ten of those who responded said they had been cyberbullied. Cyberstalking is also common. It involves using apps, social networks, and the web to obsessively follow and harass someone.

Before smartphones became popular, bullying might have taken place in person on playgrounds or in other settings. Today, bullying often happens online. It is easy for a bully to hide or be anonymous online. And with the arrival of the smartphone, communication can take place at any time. This constant accessibility has a downside. Because of this, there may be no safe zone, such as home, where someone can escape the cyberbullying. Also, it is harder for parents, teachers, or coaches to control cyberbullying because it is not as easily observed as in-person bullying.

Bystanders take photos of a protest in London, England, in 2017. Smartphones help people document protests and spread the word about important causes.

SMARTPHONES AND SOCIAL MOVEMENTS

Some people use smartphones to help organize social movements and connect with others in their communities, their countries, or around the world. Groups of people pushing for social change have used smartphones to spread the word about their causes. Arab Spring and the Occupy movement are just two examples. Arab Spring was a wave of anti-government protests that spread across the Middle East in 2011. It is sometimes referred to as the

Twitter Revolution because people used Twitter and other social media platforms to share information during the protests. The Occupy movement was a series of protests that started in the United States in 2011. People worked to raise awareness of social injustice and economic inequalities. The Occupy movement eventually spread to other countries.

In 2019, another social movement gained momentum in Hong Kong, China. Hong Kong's government is not a full democracy, but many people wanted it to be. They clashed with police in riots and protests. The protesters used smartphones and social media to organize mass demonstrations. Both the protesters and authorities used social media to try to sway public opinion in their favor.

In all these movements, smartphones and social media played a major role in how the protests unfolded. The people who organized the protests used these tools to reach out to people and quickly assemble huge crowds of protesters. In some cases, they also used these tools to educate the protesters on how to move through the cities and how to deal with the tear gas used by police to break up the crowds. Protesters used their smartphones to take videos of the protests, which they shared through social media. This allowed protesters to share news fast.

CHAPTER FOUR

HOW CAN PEOPLE CONTROL THEIR SMARTPHONE USE?

Like many things, smartphone use is good in moderation. The key is learning how to use the smartphone without giving in to the strong urge to overuse it. Science journalist Yudhijit Bhattacharjee says, "Learning to live with the technology without surrendering to it may be one of the biggest challenges we face in the digital era."[33] Achieving this balance could help smartphone users pay greater attention to their in-person relationships and improve their social interactions.

> "Learning to live with the technology without surrendering to it may be one of the biggest challenges we face in the digital era."[33]
>
> —Science journalist Yudhijit Bhattacharjee

Smartphones are a part of people's daily lives. In 2019, researchers estimated that 81 percent of US adults owned a smartphone.

Navigating a world where smartphones are nearly everywhere is a relatively new challenge. Smartphone technology is also evolving, and smartphones may have even more addictive features in the future. Many parents are concerned about their teens' smartphone habits. Some parents limit the amount of time their teens spend each day on smartphones. But it is not just teens who struggle to limit their smartphone use. Many adults overuse smartphones too.

A BALANCED APPROACH

Researchers acknowledge that smartphones are here to stay and that they have important purposes in modern society. People are able to communicate, conduct business, and have fun in new ways because of the smartphone. David Sbarra says, "We stay away from the question of whether social networking sites and smartphone use are good or bad, per se. Technology is everywhere, and it's not going away, nor should it."[34]

Researchers suggest that it helps to be specific when talking about the pros and cons of smartphone use. Amy Orben is a psychologist at the Oxford Internet Institute. She says,

Important nuance is missing if we just talk about digital technologies in general. Scrolling through skinny Instagram models will naturally have very different effects than Skyping your grandmother or chatting with your school classmates.[35]

Smartphone users should not only consider how much time they spend on their phones, but also think about the ways in which they use their phones. Smartphones can be used to form or improve relationships. They can enhance communication in many ways.

Andrew Przybylski is also a psychologist at the Oxford Internet Institute. He compares screen time to nutrition to explain how it is important to consider the context when trying to decide if smartphone use is wise. "In nutrition, you wouldn't talk about 'food time,'" Przybylski says. "You talk about calories, talk about carbohydrates, fats, and proteins—the idea of 'screen time' contains none of that richness."[36] By reviewing their smartphone habits, people can make better decisions about how and when to use these devices.

Larry Rosen is a psychologist and the author of the book *The Distracted Mind: Ancient Brains in a High-Tech World*. He says,

> *Most people check their phone every fifteen minutes or less, even if they have no alerts or notifications. We've built up this layer of anxiety surrounding our use of technology, that if we don't check in as often as we think we should, we're missing out.*[37]

Smartphone users can educate themselves about how their phones may be affecting their lives and their social interactions. They can use tools and strategies to curb or change their smartphone use.

PUSH NOTIFICATIONS

Push notifications are distracting for many smartphone users. These alerts let users know that a new message or update is available in their phone apps. Phones often announce these notifications with a buzz, a banner, or a dinging sound. Apps use these notifications to get users' attention. For example, some app notifications invite users to play games or remind them of how many steps they have taken that day. The persistent interruptions of these notifications make it hard for some users to turn away from their phones. They are constantly being pulled back to the phone screen.

In 2003, the phone company BlackBerry invented push notifications for email. Its intention was to free users from constantly checking their phones. Because of these notifications, BlackBerry phone users did not need to worry about missing an email. Users could leave their phone alone until a notification sounded, alerting them to a new email. Then in 2008, the tech company Apple created more push notification options for its iPhones. Suddenly, marketers could stay in contact with potential customers almost constantly through their smartphones. Push notifications often made smartphone users check their phones even more frequently.

Smartphone users can turn off push notifications in their phones' settings. Turning off these notifications does not cause a loss of information. It just allows users to better control when they see and access new information. Some people turn off all notifications. Others turn off notifications

for most apps but leave on a few, such as notifications for text messages. Turning off notifications is one way for smartphone users to cut down on the distractions that can interfere with their social interactions.

GRAYSCALE

Colorful smartphone app icons are appealing to users, and researchers and tech companies know this. Thomas Z. Ramsøy is a researcher who studies neurobiology and psychology. Neurobiology is the study of the nervous system, which includes the brain and nerves that send signals throughout the body. Ramsøy explores the motivations behind people's behaviors, and he helps businesses apply this research to their work. In 2018, he used brain scans and eye tracking technology to understand how people respond to smartphones and apps. Companies such as Facebook have turned to him to help them figure out ways to better draw customers' attention. Ramsøy says, "Color and shape, these are the icebreakers when it comes to grabbing people's attention. . . . Having an interface that grabs people's attention without disturbing them . . . that's the fine line."[38]

People who design smartphone apps use bright colors to attract users. Bevil Conway is a neuroscientist at the National Eye Institute. He explains how color plays a role in people's behaviors. He says, "Color's not a signal for detecting objects, it's actually something much more fundamental: It's for telling us what's likely to be important. If you have lots of color and contrast then you're under a

Developers make phone backgrounds and apps colorful to attract users' attention. Many apps have bold or bright colors.

constant state of attentional recruitment. Your attentional system is constantly going, 'Look look look over here.'"[39]

Users can reduce or dim the colors on their smartphone screens by putting their phones in grayscale mode. This option can be found in a phone's settings. It makes the phone screen appear in shades of black, white, and gray. Grayscale mode makes apps less appealing to look at. As a result, people may look at their phone less. Grayscale mode is available on smartphones that use the Android or iOS operating systems.

STOP SCROLLING

Many popular smartphone apps such as Facebook and Twitter are designed with infinite scrolling. As people scroll down a list of posts, new posts constantly load. Users can scroll endlessly, looking for an exciting post they may have missed. Human brains are designed to search for the next reward. Curiosity can be a good thing, but smartphone users may find themselves mindlessly scrolling through an app, searching for another post or feature to entertain them. When people are deeply engaged in apps, it is easy for them to miss out on in-person social interactions. To break this cycle of endless scrolling, smartphone users can choose to delete some of the apps that have this feature from their phone.

TRACK PHONE TIME

It can be easy for people to lose track of time when they are using a smartphone. David Greenfield is a professor of psychiatry at the University of Connecticut School of Medicine. He is also the founder of the Center for Internet and Technology Addiction. He routinely asks his students if they have ever lost track of time while they were online. He reported that 80 to 90 percent of his students said yes.

Some app developers have created apps to help users track the time they spend on their smartphones. Some of the most popular time-tracking apps include Social Fever, My Addictiometer, OffTime, QualityTime, App Usage, and App Detox. These apps allow users to see how much time they spend on their phones each day. Some of the apps allow users to set time limits for themselves. Another time-tracking feature in many iPhones is called Screen Time. Screen Time allows users to set time limits for

The Screen Time feature on iPhones tells users the average time they spend on their phone each day. It also breaks down how much time is spent on different types of apps, such as social networking apps.

certain apps. Users can choose to receive notifications when their time limits are reached.

MAKE A MEDIA PLAN

People who would like to limit the time they spend on their smartphones can also create media plans. Media plans are structured daily rules for phone use. The American

Academy of Pediatrics recommends that families develop family media plans. These plans could include guidelines such as no phones at the table during mealtime, no phone use during homework time, or no phone use during time spent together as a family. Every family member agrees to follow these rules. Families work together to observe the smartphone-free times of the day.

Researcher Ryan Dwyer says,

Phone use can be a bit of a habit. You're used to pulling your phone out and looking for new notifications. Have a rule that if you're going to go out to dinner with some friends or family members, you'll put your phone on silent and leave it off the table. Try to stick to these rules so you can form new habits.[40]

Media plans can help families and friends improve their relationships and their social interactions.

DIGITAL DETOX

Some people struggle with smartphone addiction. They may choose to do a digital detox. A digital detox can involve shutting down a device for a certain period of time. It can also mean staying away from a particular app, game, or tool that consumes a lot of a user's time. People who are drawn to social media might stay off social media apps for a while.

Outdoor activities such as biking can be fun alternatives to spending time on smartphones. People may avoid or restrict their use of many devices during a digital detox.

People might decide to do a digital detox if they think their smartphone or another electronic device is taking up too much of their time or causing them unwanted stress. People might benefit from a digital detox if they are anxious when they cannot find their phone, if they feel depressed after spending time on social media, if they feel they must check their phone every few minutes, or if their phone use

About one in six US adults owns a smart watch. Smart watches have apps that people can use to text, check social media, and do many other activities.

has a negative impact on their relationships. People who attempt a digital detox may find it helpful to stay busy with productive hobbies or activities to reduce the stress and anxiety of being away from their smartphones.

LOOKING TO THE FUTURE

Digital technologies continue to evolve and improve. Some digital communication devices, such as smart wearables, have replaced smartphones. Smart wearables are devices that people wear as accessories, such as smart watches. They respond to a user's voice, touch, or gesture. Amy Webb is an adjunct assistant professor of marketing at New York University's Stern School of Business. She says, "The transition from smartphones to smart wearables and invisible interfaces . . . will forever change how we experience the physical world."[41]

While smartphones are not disappearing from the market, they may look different and have many new features in the future. Advances in technology could make smartphones more attractive to users. Smartphone addiction will likely remain an issue. Users will still need to decide how to best navigate the digital world while nurturing the personal interactions that enrich their friendships, family life, and work life.

SOURCE NOTES

INTRODUCTION: SMARTPHONES AND SOCIAL INTERACTIONS

1. Valentina Rotundi, Luca Stanca, and Miriam Tomasuolo, "Connecting Alone: Smartphone Use, Quality of Social Interactions and Well-Being," *Journal of Economic Psychology*, December 2017. www.sciencedirect.com.

2. Quoted in Lynne Peeples, "Can't Put Down The Phone? How Smartphones Are Changing Our Brains—and Lives," *NBC News*, December 14, 2018. www.nbcnews.com.

3. Quoted in "FOMO: It's Your Life You're Missing Out On," *Science Daily*, March 30, 2016. www.sciencedaily.com.

4. Quoted in Yudhijit Bhattacharjee, "Smartphones Revolutionize Our Lives—But at What Cost?" *National Geographic*, January 25, 2019. www.nationalgeographic.com.

CHAPTER 1: DO SMARTPHONES AFFECT USERS' INTERACTIONS?

5. Rotundi, Stanca, and Tomasuolo, "Connecting Alone: Smartphone Use, Quality of Social Interactions and Well-Being."

6. Rotundi, Stanca, and Tomasuolo, "Connecting Alone: Smartphone Use, Quality of Social Interactions and Well-Being."

7. Quoted in Peeples, "Can't Put Down The Phone? How Smartphones Are Changing Our Brains—and Lives."

8. Quoted in "How Smartphones Are Affecting Our Relationships," *Association for Psychological Science*, February 11, 2019. www.psychologicalscience.org.

9. Bhattacharjee, "Smartphones Revolutionize Our Lives—But at What Cost?"

10. Quoted in Sarah P. Weeldreyer, "I Won't Buy My Teenagers Smartphones," *The Atlantic*, September 11, 2019. www.theatlantic.com.

11. Jean M. Twenge, "Have Smartphones Destroyed a Generation?" *The Atlantic*, September 2017. www.theatlantic.com.

12. Quoted in Twenge, "Have Smartphones Destroyed a Generation?"

13. Twenge, "Have Smartphones Destroyed a Generation?"

14. Twenge, "Have Smartphones Destroyed a Generation?"

CHAPTER 2: HOW DO SMARTPHONES AFFECT USERS' DAILY LIVES?

15. Rotundi, Stanca, and Tomasuolo, "Connecting Alone: Smartphone Use, Quality of Social Interactions and Well-Being."

16. Rotundi, Stanca, and Tomasuolo, "Connecting Alone: Smartphone Use, Quality of Social Interactions and Well-Being."

17. Rotundi, Stanca, and Tomasuolo, "Connecting Alone: Smartphone Use, Quality of Social Interactions and Well-Being."

18. Quoted in Peeples, "Can't Put Down The Phone? How Smartphones Are Changing Our Brains—and Lives."

19. Quoted in Natalia Lusinski, "12 Ways Your Smartphone Is Making Your Life Worse," *Business Insider*, June 7, 2018. www.businessinsider.com.

20. Quoted in Lusinski, "12 Ways Your Smartphone Is Making Your Life Worse."

21. Quoted in Jamie Ducharme, "Using Your Phone at Dinner Isn't Just Rude. It Also Makes You Unhappy," *Time*, February 28, 2018. www.time.com.

22. Quoted in "How Smartphones Are Affecting Our Relationships."

23. Quoted in Katherine Lee, "Why Too Much Cell Phone Usage Can Hurt Your Family Relationships," *Verywell Family*, September 16, 2019. www.verywellfamily.com.

SOURCE NOTES
CONTINUED

CHAPTER 3: HOW DO SMARTPHONES AFFECT COMMUNITIES?

24. Quoted in "How Smartphones Are Affecting Our Relationships."

25. Quoted in Lee, "Why Too Much Cell Phone Usage Can Hurt Your Family Relationships."

26. Peeples, "Can't Put Down The Phone? How Smartphones Are Changing Our Brains—and Lives."

27. Peeples, "Can't Put Down The Phone? How Smartphones Are Changing Our Brains—and Lives."

28. Yalda T. Uhls, Minas Michikyan, Jordan Morris, Debra Garcia, Gary W. Small, Eleni Zgourou, and Patricia M. Greenfield, "Five Days at Outdoor Education Camp Without Screens Improves Preteen Skills with Nonverbal Emotion Cues," *Computers in Human Behavior*, October 2014. www.sciencedirect.com.

29. Quoted in Edward Graham, "Using Smartphones in the Classroom," *National Education Association*, 2019. www.nea.org.

30. Quoted in Graham, "Using Smartphones in the Classroom."

31. Quoted in Peeples, "Can't Put Down The Phone? How Smartphones Are Changing Our Brains—and Lives."

32. Quoted in Lusinski, "12 Ways Your Smartphone Is Making Your Life Worse."

CHAPTER 4: HOW CAN PEOPLE CONTROL THEIR SMARTPHONE USE?

33. Bhattacharjee, "Smartphones Revolutionize Our Lives—But at What Cost?"

34. Quoted in "How Smartphones Are Affecting Our Relationships."

35. Quoted in Brian Resnick, "Have Smartphones Really Destroyed a Generation? We Don't Know," *Vox*, May 16, 2019. www.vox.com.

36. Quoted in Resnick, "Have Smartphones Really Destroyed a Generation? We Don't Know."

37. Quoted in Jillian D'Onfro, "These Simple Steps Will Help You Stop Checking Your Phone So Much," *CNBC*, January 3, 2018. www.cnbc.com.

38. Quoted in Nellie Bowles, "Is the Answer to Phone Addiction a Worse Phone?" *The New York Times*, January 12, 2018. www.nytimes.com.

39. Quoted in Bowles, "Is the Answer to Phone Addiction a Worse Phone?"

40. Quoted in Ducharme, "Using Your Phone at Dinner Isn't Just Rude. It Also Makes You Unhappy."

41. Quoted in Rob Lever, "After Conquering The World, Smartphone Faces Uncertain Future," *Phys.org*, November 13, 2018. www.phys.org.

FOR FURTHER RESEARCH

BOOKS

Susan Henneberg, *Are Mobile Devices Harmful?* San Diego, CA: ReferencePoint Press, 2017.

Kristin Marciniak, *Twitter*. Minneapolis, MN: Abdo Publishing, 2019.

Taylor Morris, *You're Addicted to Your Phone: How to Break the Habit*. New York: Enslow Publishing, 2019.

Bradley Steffens, *Cell Phone Addiction*. San Diego, CA: ReferencePoint Press, 2020.

Bradley Steffens, *Thinking Critically: Cell Phones*. San Diego, CA: ReferencePoint Press, 2018.

INTERNET SOURCES

Monica Anderson and Jingjing Jiang, "Teens, Social Media & Technology 2018," *Pew Research Center*, May 31, 2018. www.pewresearch.org.

"How Smartphones Are Affecting Our Relationships," *Association for Psychological Science*, February 11, 2019. www.psychologicalscience.org.

Heather Kelly, "Even Teens Think They Use Their Phones Too Much," *CNN*, August 22, 2018. www.money.cnn.com.

WEBSITES

America Offline
www.americaoffline.info

This site promotes healthy offline experiences for teens and adults. It educates people on how to balance technology use with other activities.

HelpGuide
www.helpguide.org

HelpGuide is a nonprofit organization that raises awareness of mental health issues and related topics such as smartphone addiction. Its website describes what smartphone addiction is and offers strategies for curbing smartphone use.

Psychology Today
www.psychologytoday.com

Psychology Today shares the latest research on mental health issues, including smartphone addiction. People can learn how smartphones affect users' thoughts and behaviors.

INDEX

absent presence, 27

American Academy of Pediatrics, 65–66

Android operating system, 63

App Detox, 64

App Usage, 64

Apple, 59

applications (apps), 4–8, 10–12, 17, 20, 42–49, 51, 58–65, 66

Arab Spring, 52–53

Baylor University, 36–37

Bhattacharjee, Yudhijit, 18, 54

BlackBerry, 59

California State University, Dominguez Hills, 43

Carr, Nicholas, 15

cellularitis, 40

Center for Internet and Technology Addiction, 63–64

Common Sense Media, 14, 16, 48, 50, 51

conflict resolution, 49

Conway, Bevil, 61–62

cyberbullying, 50–51

cyberstalking, 50–51

digital detox, 66–68

distractions, 6, 8–9, 17–18, 21, 23, 27–28, 33–37, 47, 58–63

dopamine, 32

Dunn, Elizabeth, 33–34, 64

Dwyer, Ryan, 33–34, 66

educational apps, 45–47

Facebook, 61, 63

FaceTime, 7

family time, 6–7, 9, 11, 34–37, 64, 66

fear of missing out (FOMO), 9

Flores, Suzana E., 31–32, 49

Gazzaley, Adam, 31

grayscale mode, 61–63

Greenfield, David, 63–64

GuardChild, 50

Halla, Ken, 44–47

health care, 47–48

Hong Kong, China, 53

Illinois State University, 14

in-person interactions, 9, 15, 17–19, 26, 27–31, 32, 48–49, 54, 63

Instagram, 6, 56

International Business Machines (IBM), 19

internet, 12, 19, 49–51

iOS operating system, 63

iPads, 21

iPhones, 21, 59, 64

Kross, Ethan, 9

Kushlev, Kostadin, 40, 48

life satisfaction, 29–31

McDaniel, Brandon, 14

McLaughlin, Darlene, 9

mealtimes, 6–7, 33–35, 64, 66

media plans, 65–66

My Addictiometer, 64

neuroscientists, 31, 61

nomophobia, 14–15

nonverbal cues, 19–20, 26

notifications, 27, 32, 43, 44, 58–60, 65–66

Occupy movement, 52–53

OffTime, 64

online interactions, 19–20, 31, 50–51

Orben, Amy, 56

Oxford Internet Institute, 56–57

parents, 6–7, 10, 14, 50–51, 55

Peeples, Lynne, 40–41

Pew Research Center, 13, 15, 21, 22

phone stack, 64

phubbing, 21, 26, 28, 31–33, 36, 40

Przybylski, Andrew, 57

psychologists, 8, 9, 16, 19, 26, 28, 31, 36, 38–40, 43, 48, 49, 56–58, 61, 63, 64

QualityTime, 64

Ramsøy, Thomas Z., 61

relationships, 14, 15–19, 23, 26, 27, 31–37, 38–39, 49, 54, 57, 66, 68

researchers, 7, 12–14, 21, 22, 24, 27–31, 33–37, 38–41, 43, 48, 56, 61, 64, 66

Roberts, James, 36–37, 40

Rosen, Larry, 43, 58

Rotondi, Valentina, 7, 12–13, 24–26, 28–31

San Diego State University, 8

Sbarra, David, 16, 36, 38–39, 56

Screen Time, 64–65

scrolling, 63

Seppälä, Emma, 26

Simon Personal Communicator, 19

Skype, 56

smart wearables, 69

smartphones
addiction, 14, 25, 31–33, 55, 57, 66–69
in businesses, 42–44
in schools, 44–47

Snapchat, 4, 20

Snapstreaks, 20

Social Fever, 64

social media, 4–6, 9, 10, 12, 16–17, 20, 26, 43, 47, 48–53, 61, 63, 66–67

social movements, 52–53

social networking, 12, 16, 51, 56

social networks, 15

social skills, 41

students, 4–5, 43, 44–47, 57, 64

studies, 13, 14, 18, 20–21, 28–31, 33–36, 40–41, 43, 61

surveys, 13–15, 16, 21, 22, 36–37, 48, 50, 51

technoference, 14

technological advances, 38–39, 69

teenagers, 10, 13–15, 16–19, 20–24, 48, 50–51, 55, 57

texting, 4–7, 11, 26, 34, 37, 45–47, 51, 60

time-tracking apps, 64–65

Twenge, Jean, 8–9, 19, 20–21, 23
Twitter, 53, 63

Uhls, Yalda, 41
University of Arizona, 16
University of British Columbia, 33
University of California, Los
    Angeles, 41
University of California, San
    Francisco, 31
University of Essex, 27
University of Kent's School of
    Psychology, 28
University of Michigan, 9
University of Oxford, 7

video chat, 7, 11–12, 20
video lectures, 47
videoconferencing, 43

web browsers, 19
Webb, Amy, 69
withdrawal symptoms, 33

IMAGE CREDITS

Cover: © antoniodiaz/Shutterstock Images

5: © Monkey Business Images/Shutterstock Images

6: © bokan/Shutterstock Images

8: © Jirapong Manustrong/Shutterstock Images

11: © SpeedKingz/Shutterstock Images

12: © LDprod/Shutterstock Images

17: © Rommel Canlas/Shutterstock Images

22: © Red Line Editorial

25: © Monkey Business Images/Shutterstock Images

29: © zhu difeng/Shutterstock Images

30: © Daisy Daisy/Shutterstock Images

35: © Syda Productions/Shutterstock Images

39: © monkeybusinessimages/iStockphoto

42: © eXpose/Shutterstock Images

45: © Iakov Filimonov/Shutterstock Images

46: © Piotr Swat/Shutterstock Images

52: © 1000 words/Shutterstock Images

55: © Meinzahn/iStockphoto

60: © Syda Productions/Shutterstock Images

62: © Vasin Lee/Shutterstock Images

65: © Cristian Dina/Shutterstock Images

67: © Jacek Chabraszewski/Shutterstock Images

68: © Monkey Business Images/Shutterstock Images

ABOUT THE AUTHOR

Donna B. McKinney is the author of more than ten nonfiction books for kids on topics ranging from science and technology to history and sports. Some of those titles include *STEM in Snowboarding*, *Careers for Tech Girls in Graphic Design*, *Getting to Know JavaScript*, *It's Great to Be a Fan in North Carolina*, and *Excelling in Soccer*. Before she wrote for children, she spent many years writing about science and technology topics such as chemistry, space science, and robotics at the US Naval Research Laboratory in Washington, DC. She has a bachelor's degree in English from Campbell University and a master's degree in English: Professional Writing and Editing from George Mason University. She lives in North Carolina.